Selected Poems:

Rosemary Dobson

Study notes for Area of Study:
Discovery 2015–2018 HSC

Julie Turk and Alex Sidoroff

Five Senses Education Pty Ltd
2/195 Prospect Highway
Seven Hills 2147
New South Wales
Australia

First Published 2014

Turk, Julie and Sidoroff, Alex
Top Notes – Rosemary Dobson
ISBN 978 -1- 74130 – 164 – 9

CONTENTS

Top Notes Series....................iv

Area Of Study: Discovery....................1

Why Study Poetry?....................26

The Composer....................31

Context....................34

Reading Journal....................36

'Young Girl At A Window'....................38

'Wonder'....................44

'Painter Of Antwerp'....................51

'Traveller's Tale'....................58

'The Tiger'....................68

'Cock Crow'....................73

'Ghost Town: New England'....................79

The Essay....................92

HSC Style Essay Question....................94

Discovery: Other Related Texts....................96

TOP NOTES SERIES

This series has been created to assist HSC students of English in their understanding of set texts. Top Notes are easy to read, provide analysis of issues and discuss important ideas contained in the texts.

Particular care has been taken to ensure that students are able to examine each text in the context of the area of study or module to which it has been allocated.

Each text generally includes:

- Notes on the specific module
- Plot summary
- Character analysis
- Setting
- Thematic concerns
- Language studies
- Essay questions and a modelled response
- Other textual material
- Practice questions
- Useful quotes

We have covered the areas we feel are important for students in their study of Discovery for their Area of Study. I am sure you will find these Top Notes useful in your studies of English.

Bruce Pattinson
Series Editor

AREA OF STUDY: DISCOVERY

'We learn wisdom from failure much more than from success. We often discover what will do, by finding out what will not do; and probably he who never made a mistake never made a discovery.'

SAMUEL SMILES

The Area of Study set for the 2015–18 HSC is *Discovery*. It is compulsory to study this topic as prescribed by the Board of Studies. Remember you are supposed to analyse your texts with reference to varying aspects of *Discovery*. Markers will be looking to see evidence of deep conceptual understanding of the Area of Study and you are encouraged to support your views with close textual referencing.

In the Area of Study you will be analysing many texts that are related to the idea of discovery. You will analyse texts not only to investigate the ideas they present about this area but also how they deliver these ideas. This means you will be looking closely at the techniques composers use to represent ideas and shape meaning. You will also be looking at relationships between texts. Overall, you will become an expert on discovery- the different notions people have about it and the various ways composers manipulate techniques to communicate their ideas about the topic. The material in this Top Note will help you do that.

Specifically you will look at:

- A set text from the following list of fourteen texts. **You will only study one of these.**
  - *Wrack* – James Bradley
  - *The Awakening* – Kate Chopin
  - *A Short History of Nearly Everything* – Bill Bryson
  - *The Motorcycle Diaries* – Ernesto 'Che' Guevara
  - *Swallow the Air* – Tara June Winch
  - *Away* – Michael Gow
  - *Rainbow's End* – Jane Harrison
  - *Frank Hurley - The Man Who Made History* – Simon Nasht
  - *Life of Pi* – Ang Lee
  - *The Tempest* – William Shakespeare
  - *Selected Poems* – Robert Gray
  - *Selected Poems* – Rosemary Dobson
  - *Selected Poems* – Robert Frost
  - *Go Back To Where You Came From* – selected episodes – Ivan O'Mahoney
- Additional related texts of your own choosing.

You must write about your set text and additional texts of your own choosing in the first English paper of the HSC examination.

> *I hope that posterity will judge me kindly, not only as to the things which I have explained, but also to those which I have intentionally omitted so as to leave to others the pleasure of discovery.*
>
> **RENE DESCARTES**

WHAT DOES THE BOARD OF STUDIES REQUIRE FOR THE AREA OF STUDY?

The Board of Studies documentation says of the Area of Study: Discovery that it;

'requires students to explore the ways in which the concept of discovery is represented in and through texts.' (p 9)

The document English Stage 6 Prescriptions: Area of Study Electives and Texts (August 2013) notes that perceptions of discovery can encompass many things and are shaped by context.

- Students can consider –not only discovery but also rediscovery.
- That discovery may be planned or unplanned and may lead to new worlds and values.
- Discoveries can question and challenge and lead to different conclusions.

You will also need to consider that the 'process of discovering can vary according to personal, cultural, historical and social contexts and values.'

Below is an abbreviated version of what the Board requires of students.

'In their responses and compositions students examine, question, reflect and speculate on':

- their own experiences of discovery, personally and through texts.

- the assumptions underlying the representations of discovery.
- the effects of composers' choices of techniques.
- the ways in which the study of discovery has helped them understand the world and themselves.

Think carefully about the wording that is used so that you can adopt this language for your own work.

If this is what is required by the Board of Studies you need to examine the concept of discovery carefully so you can respond adequately. We would recommend that you read the complete document which is on the Board of Studies website (http://www.bostes.nsw.edu.au) and can be downloaded in Word or PDF formats.

UNDERSTANDING THE AREA OF STUDY

'There is no better high than discovery'

- E. O. WILSON

Discovery is often associated with adventure. The word *Discovery* conjures childhood dreams of exotic locations, intrepid explorers in jungles discovering lost tribes and great treasures. Movies embrace this theme. The Discovery Channel exists to help people to discover facts vicariously. The concept behind the never-ending Star Trek series is to 'explore strange new worlds, to seek out new life and new civilisations, to boldly go where no man has gone before'.

Even the self-discovery / self-help industry is a major one in all the nations of earth; people are willing to make great sacrifices to discover the 'truth' about themselves and the world. All this is undoubtedly true but discovery is much more than this and we will need to have a broader and more sophisticated understanding to undertake our studies of the texts set for study.

The Board of Studies has outlined in their documentation: students are required to 'explore the ways in which the concept of discovery is represented in and through texts'. (p 9 *HSC Prescriptions 2015–20 English Stage 6*). This is our first step and it indicates that we must pay particular attention to the text and its content and techniques, particularly the techniques the composer uses to engage the audience and convey the main purpose of their text.

The whole aim of this Area of Study is to examine the text closely but also relate it to the idea of discovery and decide how examining it in this way enables us to better understand both the text and the concept. It is important that you formulate your own ideas about the text and attempt to develop some original and creative ideas about what you are studying.

The Board's documentation should be read in full and the annotations document should also be examined for the particular texts you are studying as this document offers insights into the way each particular text should be examined by outlining key ideas and areas for clarification.

The *Prescriptions* document states on the Area of Study that *Discovery* can be:

- something new
- a rediscovery
- sudden, unexpected
- carefully planned
- 'fresh and intensely meaningful in ways that may be emotional, creative, intellectual, physical and spiritual.' (p 9)

- confronting
- provocative
- enable speculation

It can:

- change perceptions of individuals and groups.
- create new values

The document also suggests that discoveries and ways of discovering vary due to individual circumstance and that these discoveries can change many things about lives, communities and the world(s). Of course when we examine the concept of discovery we need to examine how 'discovering' the text itself may change us and how we view things. The text may challenge and confront and change how we see the human experience.

Students can also think about 'their own experiences of discovery' and how a composer's choice of form, feature and language influences their views of discovery. Examining and enjoying any text is a discovery in itself but it is what we take away from the text and apply that is the real discovery. That is not to say that every text will be enjoyed or offer a discovery. Some may not personally engage you and that is fine. This is especially so when you begin to find other related material that links to Discovery. Find examples of texts that link in significant ways to your prescribed text.

Defining Discovery

'Definition is the death of discovery'

-TOM SHADYAK

Now let's define discovery in a more coherent and easily understood way so we can begin our investigation at a basic level before moving into more complex analysis. Dictionary.com defines the term as:

1. The act or instance of discovering

2. Something discovered

3. In legal terms it is compulsory disclosure of evidence

4. The name of the third space shuttle.

Obviously the first three terms are more suitable but the final definition shows how pervasive the idea of discovery is and how it has influenced people over time. The search for the 'new' has driven much development over past millennia. Discoveries are always met with excitement and often trepidation as to what change they might bring.

Think historically about how people have reacted to change. It can cause great upheavals in society, with violent reactions while other changes brought through discoveries are welcomed and may save and enhance lives. Consider medical advancements, scientific developments and the ever-quickening world of the computer. Even the way I am creating this text in Evernote on an iPad would not have been possible twelve months ago. Discovery brings change and may affect different people or groups of people, even nations in various ways both positive and negative. It is pertinent now to examine some more definitions.

The word discover and its definition also sheds some light on the concept:

1. To see, get knowledge, to learn, to find, get knowledge of something previously seen or unknown.

As does the definition of the word discovering:

1. Noticing or realising.

These definitions all point to the fact that realisation is the key to discovery. This realisation may come unexpectedly, occasionally or never. Someone else may have the same experience and make the discovery. The realisation may be accidental or organised, take years in the planning or come as a complete surprise.

Discoveries can come in many ways and the synonyms for discover listed below help us to understand the concept even further. They assist in defining how a discovery can arise:

Synonyms – ascertain, catch, come upon, contrive, determine, design, dig up, disclose, elicit, explore, bring to light, unearth, encounter, experiment, invent, originate, expose, locate, perceive, sense, strike, verify.

These synonyms show partly the vast array of words that our language has created around this concept and show how important it is in the human psyche. Look also at the antonyms that show how we view not discovering things; lose, miss, pass by.

We, as a race, want to discover. Now we will look at some examples of discovery and examine their impact. It is also important to remember that discoveries do not have to be positive. You might discover you have a huge problem, an incurable illness, a strange past, an unwelcome relative or something equally bizarre. There may be a darker side to any discovery that could be addressed. Think about the effect of the white discoverers on indigenous populations.

Types of Discovery

Personal Discovery

'I think a spiritual journey is not so much a journey of discovery. It's a journey of recovery. It's a journey of uncovering your own inner nature. It's already there.'

BILLY CORGAN

The idea of personal discovery or self-discovery as many of the books also describe it, is a popular and pervasive concept. It is more prevalent in the developed nations of the world where people seek something more spiritual or meaningful rather than their consumer driven lives and the day to day grind of work. Many seek something more; they strive to discover something within or without, a better self, a way to live in the now or just a way to escape from reality. A huge amount of material (literature, DVDs, audiobooks) has been assembled to help individuals achieve their life goals.

Individuals seek to achieve personal discovery in a variety of ways. Some examples are courses and conferences where they are led through exercises, both physical and psychological, to develop new skills and discover their inner spirituality. Others join communities, religious groups or renounce material possessions and become itinerant travellers or, in old fashioned terms, 'hippies'. Through this they discover whatever they lack in their current state (hopefully) and become a better or more effective person. Others use these discoveries to enrich themselves or manage better in their existing lives. Whatever the reason or outcome, personal discovery is a huge industry and an integral part of our society.

For more information on this area you could investigate the self-help, self- improvement section of a book store or get on YouTube and type these terms in. You will get plenty of ideas and advice!

Inner Discovery

'The greatest discovery of my generation is that man can alter his life simply by altering his attitude of mind.'

JAMES ADAMS

The concept of inner discovery is closely aligned with the previous topic and can be seen similarly yet it is more aligned with exceptional circumstances. For example some people learn much about themselves during physical, emotional or psychologically stressful times and are astounded by the inner strength they have while others around them break down or fail to cope. Others find inner strength through meditation, retreats, or extremes such as becoming a hermit and focusing on the inner person. This concept of personal enlightenment is also a business in the modern world and you can get coaches who will work with you to find your inner self through various processes of discovery.

If you are looking for examples to use in your related material try googling the term and you will find a whole range of programs, coaches and books that will help you find your inner self. Dag Hammarskjold (former UN Secretary General) said 'The longest journey is the journey inwards. Of him who has chosen his destiny, who has started upon his quest for the source of his being.'

Discovery through Travel

The idea of discovery through travel is one of the first things that occur to people when they hear the word discovery. As Martin Buber (Austrian-born 20th Century Jewish philosopher) stated, 'All journeys have secret destinations of which the traveller is unaware'. This sense of travel enabling discoveries is well documented and became even more prominent as people began to sail widely across the seas to discover 'new' lands, many of which had been occupied by indigenous peoples for centuries. Travel was, and to some extent still is, associated with an adventure, a journey, to test the boundaries of what we already know and to see how far we can take the new experience and how it changes us. What we discover on our travels is revealing and often confronting.

> *Adventure is a path. Real adventure—self-determined, self-motivated, often risky—forces you to have firsthand encounters with the world. The world the way it is, not the way you imagine it. Your body will collide with the earth and you will bear witness. In this way you will be compelled to grapple with the limitless kindness and bottomless cruelty of humankind—and perhaps realise that you yourself are capable of both. This will change you. Nothing will ever again be black-and-white.*
>
> **– MARK JENKINS**
>
> **(HTTP://MATADORNETWORK.COM/BNT/50-MOST-INSPIRING-TRAVEL-QUOTES-OF-ALL-TIME/#RCM3GIDFTO4PO7MB.99)**

Discovery through travel brings this kind of change and it may involve understanding another culture, disrupting a prejudice or habit, making a friend or discovering some amazing natural beauty. Discovery through travel is one of the most written about and frequently mentioned ideas when discussing the concept. Travel has certainly changed over the centuries, even in the past decade travel to distant places has become commonplace. Air travel has especially become less than the special thing for the privileged or extremely adventurous that it was in the beginning. Think back to the times when to travel from place to place by foot or by horse was a major event. From the Middle Ages through to the later eighteenth century many people had never ventured beyond their village, apart from an infrequent trip to the nearest town. This idea leads us to consider the idea of the journey.

Discovery through Journey

This is an idea common to many areas of the discovery concept. Often the two words are associated if we think of the journey as a process not just a physical movement. Often discoveries are made on the journey rather than at the destination. The word journey has also been applied to abstract concepts. Lyndon Johnson, the American President, described peace as a deliberate process: 'Peace is a journey of a thousand miles and it must be taken one step at a time'. Many have heard the quote by Lao Tzu 'A journey of a thousand miles must begin with one step'.

The concept of journey leading to discovery is a constant in modern film and literature and it has been extensively studied in works such as Joseph Campbell's *The Hero's Journey*. This model organises the journey by stages which are common to all culture. Despite the cross-cultural commonalities, journeys allow discovery about self and such discoveries are individual.

As Marcel Proust (19th and 20th Century French novelist) stated, 'We don't receive wisdom; we must discover it for ourselves after a journey that no one can take for us or spare us.'

The physical journey could be local, in the same country, overseas or even in space, a place many science fiction texts take us. Fantasy writers create journeys of discovery in worlds of imagination and invention. Film also focuses on the concept of discovery through journey as we see in the range of road trip movies that seem so appealing to teen audiences. More serious films examine personal independence, the human condition and how one can discover something on the journey that will change or even save humanity. You will find many examples of this in film but try and choose something where the discovery has some significant personal and/or social impact and you can discuss techniques. Consider the idea of the journey as being inextricably linked to the concept of discovery as you make your way through the Area of Study.

Scientific and Technological Discovery

'Scientists have become the bearers of the torch of discovery in our quest for knowledge'

STEPHEN HAWKING

Regarding areas of discovery, foremost in many people's thoughts are the breakthroughs made in science and technology. They have immediate and significant impacts on modern day individuals and the way they interface with the world.

Examples of the impact of technology include:

- increased internet usage leading to the rise of social networking.
- miniaturisation of hand-held devices such as the iPad enabling people to communicate easily and more often.

- rapid changes in the way that data is stored such as the increased use of cloud-storage services has facilitated the development of much more flexible devices.

Einstein pointed out 'The process of scientific discovery is, in effect, a flight from wonder.' This is central to much of the debate that has raged over science in the past century or so. How do we progress scientifically and technologically and still maintain a moral and ethical basis? Should we chase many of the ideas that have arisen? For example the machines of war, the chemicals that kill and the genetic manipulations that can lead to social engineering are discoveries with ethical implications. Should there be limits and controls and if so how much? Discoveries can be fraught with danger on many levels.

While it is part of discovery to imagine and test the boundaries and seek new ways, it is also probably integral to human nature. With these new technologies the consequences are even greater than in the past as more people can be affected, more invasively and quickly. Dangers emerge as people discover new methods of being destructive, such as invading computers to distort programs with viruses or stealing through cybercrimes. These examples highlight that discoveries are not always positive.

Humanity must also grapple with the discovery of things such as climate change and environmental issues that are the result of industrialisation through discovered technologies. The consequences of many of the discoveries in the latter half of the last century are still being felt and new discoveries are needed to solve these problems. Discovery can be cyclical, inter-related and never-ending. Google '2014 Shift Happens' and watch a YouTube clip highlighting the rapid rate of discovery and change in this modern era!

Discovery as Creating New From Old

This is an intriguing idea probably best summed up in the idea of recycling materials to create something new. Old tyres can be used as soft fall for children's playgrounds, old ideas can be given new form, new ways can be thought up to approach a topic. Even just drawing attention to a common feature can enable people to discover something about it. This form of discovery is seen as creativity.

One example might be the light show Vivid which featured in Sydney. Prominent buildings such as the Opera House were illuminated with an exciting coloured light show. The buildings around the harbour foreshores were visible and bathed in psychedelic colours. People flocked to see the spectacle and the show received great reviews. The reactions evoked by the light show captured the idea of discovery and re-invention as otherwise familiar images were seen in an entirely new way. The sense of wonder and amazement experienced by young children observing the show was evidence of their discovery.

Sometimes a newly discovered thing can be as simple as reading a novel previously read or re-watching a film seen years before and getting something new or different from it. Great artists always borrow from the past and rearrange old elements into new discoveries for their audiences. Ideas such as this have led to new movements in the Arts or new methods of approaching a topic that casts new light on it. Postmodern texts such as the film *The Matrix*, use intertextuality as a key aspect.

Learning as Discovery

Learning in itself is a discovery that can make significant changes to an individual or a group. When we learn something that can be applied it is a small but potentially significant discovery for the individual or group. One significant piece of learning was the manipulation of fire, another the growing of crops, developing shelter and so on. While these are major discoveries other learning can be especially important for the individual. One example might be a breakthrough in reading or the ability to analyse and manipulate information to create something new. Consider this aspect of discovery as it can link to the other areas and be useful as an overriding idea to utilise as a thesis for the Area of Study essay.

Detection as Discovery

> *The basis of drama is... The struggle of the hero toward a specific goal at the end of which he realises that what kept him from it was, in the lesser drama, civilisation and, in the greater drama, the discovery of something that he did not set out to discover but which can be seen retrospectively as inevitable.*
>
> **DAVID MAMET**

The concept of detection as discovery is the integral aspect of the success of the eternally popular crime fiction genre and is also a major aspect of thrillers and similar literature, film and the visual arts. Paintings, for example, prove excellent material, to demonstrate how an individual can deduce something different from the same work as the person next to them. Detection, however, in its truest form is highly valued by audiences as it is about discovering the truth through clues.

Much literature has been written in this quest to make sense of a world where justice sometimes appears to be lacking. Of course the detective genre has changed much over the years and these variations have come to suit changing audiences and contexts but this search has rarely varied despite the form in which it is presented. Audiences love the sense of discovery in detection and an examination of any television or film guide will attest to the fact, as will an examination of library bookshelves.

"HOLMES GAVE ME A SKETCH OF THE EVENTS."

The Psychology of Discovery

'There'll always be serendipity involved in discovery'

JEFF BUZOS

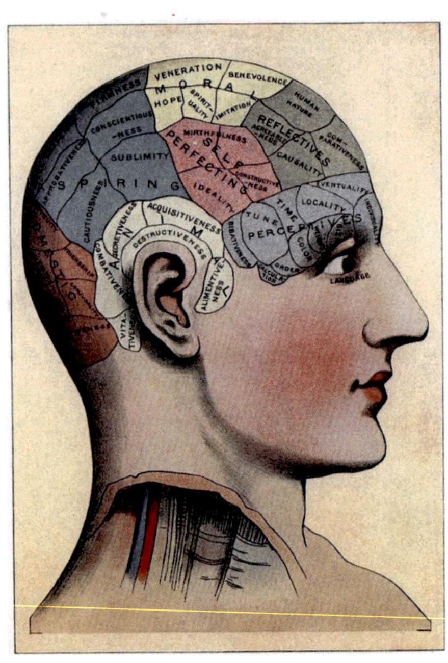

When I alluded to the innate need for discovery in the human psyche it wasn't superficial. The need for humanity to move ahead, to discover and to break boundaries is an important part of humanity's development and seems ingrained in us. The push to conquer new boundaries, to test, to push, to break boundaries is inherent in all development. Even if the discovery is the taste of a new food, the thrill of a new friend, or the discovery of any other sensory pleasure, it is a pleasure psychologically important to human development. The American writer Pearl S. Buck, who died in 1973, said that the basic discovery is the 'discovery of the relationship between men and women.' This is still true today. This quote could be used to explore the concept of discovery and to justify textual analysis from the perspective of feminist literary criticism. The field of Literary Criticism and new readings of texts is an example of boundary breaking.

There is something basic at an emotional level about discovery that attracts us to it. The new is important, broadening and thought provoking and this affects us on a psychological level. It is the emotional response that keeps people seeking the new, to discover and to absorb. This concept of the impact of discovery on our psyche is important as it is also a useful link to each of the texts and to your related material. It may be a useful concept to enable you to link your ideas together. Think about the basic psychological drives that motivate us and how they are important in all our discoveries.

Nationalism, Capitalism and other 'isms' as Drivers of Discovery

'People acting in their own self-interest is the fuel for all the discovery, innovation, and prosperity that powers the world'

JOHN STOSSEL

The idea that the 'isms' are drivers of discovery may not be appealing to some but there is no doubt that many of the discoveries of the last few centuries have been driven by them. One example is the race to land on the moon or the space race. This led to some awesome discoveries yet was driven by the great Cold War divide between the Communist Russian dictatorship and the American capitalist democratic system. Buoyed by the need to be first to set foot on the moon and discover what was there, billions were spent in making this happen.

Earlier still, the drive by nations such as Spain, Portugal and England to colonise the 'New World', particularly Africa and the Americas, led to many discoveries. National pride here was mixed with the drive for resources to support their ideology: religious, capitalist, communist or nationalist. This also led to many negatives such as exploitation in the race to conquer lands and spread 'civilisation'.

Capitalism, whatever your political belief, has been one of the greatest engines to drive discoveries over the centuries. This striving to produce product faster, more efficiently and thus, cheaply, has driven much innovation, prompted development of new technologies and resulted in new products. The instinct to improve and achieve is driven to its purest form by the capitalist system. It is not prudent here to discuss the pros and cons of the system itself but rather to recognise that it is a consummate motivator to Discovery. Gordon Gecko's quote from the film, *Wall Street*, sums up this philosophy brilliantly,

> *'Greed is right, greed works. Greed clarifies, cuts through and captures the essence of the evolutionary spirit. Greed in all of its forms; greed for life, for money, for love, knowledge has marked the upward surge of mankind.'*

Again relevant to this is the consideration of further analysing texts through the lens of literary criticism. For example, Marxist and New Historicist readings present different interpretations and may offer responders new insights and discoveries regarding texts.

Negative Aspects of Discovery

While it is common to have a positive image of discovery it is important to remember that it has negative aspects as well. For example, many of the early explorers who set out to discover new lands ended up dead. History is littered with such examples and many have gone down as glorious failures. One example is the story of Burke and Wills in Australia but you could also examine the exploration of the Antarctic and Arctic which have many failed expeditions. Other negatives can be found in the concept of discovering dreams of riches such as El Dorado or King Solomon's Mines.

The 'discovery' of new lands by European adventurers led to the exploitation of discovered natural resources. Indigenous peoples, considered uneducated savages, were often enslaved. The 'slave trade' was a negative by-product of this period of exploitation and discovery.

Away from this idea of exploration we can also have negatives in discoveries which yield promise such as nuclear power. This 'clean fuel' has been used for destructive purposes and Oppenheimer has said of his team's creation of the atomic bomb that it was a mistake. Many discoveries have been used negatively in war and in commerce for power and/or gain. We have even experienced psychological discoveries being used for brainwashing and other pernicious purposes. We have also mentioned the 'isms' that drive discovery and these can be negatively used as well. Communism killed millions and enslaved nations, patriotism in its extreme can lead to discovery but has impacted negatively on native populations and led to war.

Remember when you select a text for your related material or study a text there may be negatives to engage with that will enhance your understanding of the concept of discovery. Look for them to broaden your knowledge and ability to write clearly and formulate your own opinions.

Afterword on Discovery

'The pace of discovery is going unbelievably fast'

JAMES WATSON

Discovery is also about **possibility**, the idea that something in an imagination can be made real and attainable. Discovery is sometimes seeing the obvious and making use of it. Above all it entails faith/dreaming and an insatiable curiosity. When you read about many discoveries they are truly tales of failure with one success. Many stories tell of years of pain, toil, ridicule, dismal progress and rejection before success is achieved. Edison made a thousand bulbs before he got one to work. Failure is a constant with many people you will study in this topic until they discover their dream. They maintained their faith in the face of great adversity and this is what makes them discoverers. If it were easy everyone would do it!

Discoverers are also people who see what others have missed. Often they simply look at something in a new way. To look for new ideas, we must maintain an open mind. To discover for ourselves the mysteries of texts and how to unlock them, we must develop strategies for analysis and perseverance to achieve understanding.

Perhaps you think everything has been discovered as a pessimist might, but discoverers are optimists, people who continually seek success, or insight in achieving their goals or realising their dreams.

Questions for Discovery

- Define the term 'discovery' in your own words.
- How can discovery and possibility be connected?
- Discuss what the term discovery means to you.
- Create your own list of synonyms and antonyms for the word discovery. Then, choose two or three to use in your writing so the word discovery won't be repeated.
- Science is often connected with discovery. Research one such instance and write two paragraphs on it connecting it thematically to your set text.
- What is positive about discovery?
- Discuss the idea that discovery can be a two-edged sword.
- Discuss one discovery and the benefits of that discovery to humanity.
- Do you think the concept of discovery is integral to detective fiction? Explain your answer fully.
- Analyse one 'ism' and how discovery has been driven by it.
- Discuss some of the negatives associated with the concept of discovery.

WHY STUDY POETRY?

Poetry is about life. It deals concisely with all the emotions arising from living and topics concerning life such as love, death, nature, friendship, feelings of pain, anger and frustration. All the moods and ideas that are part of the human condition can be seen in poetry. Poetry appeals to our understanding through our imagination and utilises sensory imagery to help us see what the poet has seen, hear what the poet has heard and to experience the poet's feelings.

Useful Terms

Familiarity with the following poetic devices and techniques will enable you to convince your examiner that you have acquired the vocabulary necessary to discuss how the composer attempts to share his or her ideas and raise aspects of discovery through the poetry. Do not forget to provide examples, explain techniques and link your analysis to the Area of Study.

Alliteration	repetition of initial consonant sounds close together – for a special/poetic sound effect/emphasis (e.g. "one <u>s</u>ummer'<u>s</u> evening <u>s</u>oaked").
Allusion	a reference to something from history, literature, religion that adds meaning.
Analysis	close examination involving taking apart for the purpose of greater understanding.

Anaphora	use of successive phrases or lines beginning with the same words. The repetition can be a single word or entire phrase. It is seen in speeches, religious and devotional poetry, including numerous Biblical Psalms.
Assonance	repetition of vowel sounds in words or lines close together.
Cliché	word or phrase which is very common and overused.
Climax	where emotions/ideas reach their peak.
Criticism	evaluation of literature, finding strong points which support the meaning and looking at style and language use.
Dissonance	harsh sounding words together for a special effect and emphasis.
Dramatic Monologue	a poetic form using one voice and often revealing much about the speaker.
Ekphrasis	a text based on a visual text, often a work of art, and offering new ways of seeing.
Enjambment	run-on-lines, with no punctuation pauses, creating a flow-on effect in the poem.

Free verse	a disregard for traditional rhyme/rhythm rules.
Hyperbole	over exaggeration for effect/emphasis (e.g. 'millionth person').
Imagery	figures of speech –such as metaphors and similes that make word pictures, comparisons or contrasts, to aid understanding (e.g. "the melting west is striped liked ice-cream").
Irony	a reversal of expected ideas used to make an effect, to draw attention to a point.
Juxtaposition	two contrasting ideas close together for dramatic effect and emphasis (e.g. "superb in silk" compared to "the Head in humbler black").
Lyric	a poem that expresses emotions and ideas.
Metaphor	a direct comparison between two things, referring to one in terms of another – without using 'like' or 'as.'
Mood	overall emotional effect/feeling set in a line or stanza of a poem.
Motif	dominant theme/object that comes up several times in a poem or collection of poems.

Narrative	style of writing which relates to a story.
Onomatopoeia	words that imitate sounds. Used for sound effect and emphasis.
Paradox	a seeming contradiction which actually is true.
Personification	to give human qualities to non-living things (e.g. "all the sun's disciples cloaked").
Realism	make vividly real by careful attention to detail.
Satire	criticise by means of subtle ridicule, with comic effect.
Simile	comparison of two unlike things, used to describe something more vividly, using 'like' or 'as'.
Stanza	divisions within a poem, similar to paragraphs in prose.
Structure	the shape or form of a text, the way it is pieced together.
Style	interplay of structure/ language/ tone that supports the theme.

Subject matter	this refers to the content of the text rather than the message.
Symbol	an image that stands for a complex idea.
Theme	central message/meaning of a piece of writing.
Tone	overall attitude conveyed by the composer to the audience. It is achieved through the combination of subject, mood and style.
Transferred epithet	figurative language where an idea is passed from one thing onto another for dramatic immediacy.

THE COMPOSER

While background on composers can help responders understand texts, be aware that examiners will expect you to engage closely with the actual text set for study.

Rosemary Dobson was born in Sydney in 1920. Her father, Arthur Dobson, was an English engineer. Her grandfather, Austin Dobson, was an acclaimed English poet although Rosemary was not aware of his achievements until she was eleven. This was after she had written her first poems. (She began to write poetry, at seven.)

Rosemary's father died when she was just five years old, leaving her mother Marjorie to raise Rosemary and her older sister Ruth. When Rosemary was nine, an aunt on her father's side visited. Due to connections, Marjorie was offered a live-in 'house mistress' position at Frensham School in Mittagong. At first the school would only take one of her daughters so Marjorie rejected the offer, but a subsequent offer, which included schooling for both daughters, was accepted.

Rosemary Dobson remained at the progressive Winifred West school, Frensham, for the entirety of her schooling. At seventeen, Dobson self-published her first book of poems. She stayed on at the school as an assistant to the Art teacher, and worked with another staff assistant called Joan Phipson, who had also been a student at the school. Phipson became an award winning Australian children's writer.

Phipson set up Frensham Press and it was on this press that Dobson's first collection of poems was printed. Phipson and even the Woolfs, with their Hogarth Press in London, were influences in Dobson's life as she became involved in the process of not only writing, but proofing and printing.

Rosemary Dobson received an inheritance from her grandfather which she used to finance a move to Sydney and attendance at Sydney University. She took classes in English, Art and Design. The renowned Australian painter Thea Proctor taught her drawing. Elegance, strength, discrimination and balance were important factors which Dobson saw in Proctor's work and which she saw as relevant in the creation of her own poetry. Critics later validated and discussed these qualities in her poetry.

When she was twenty-one Dobson got a job as a proof reader with Sydney publishers Angus and Robertson. Her first professionally published book of poetry, *In a Convex Mirror,* came out in 1944. In 1948 she won the Sydney Morning Herald prize for poetry.

Further publications followed: *The Ship of Ice* (1948), *Child with a Cockatoo* (1955) and *Cock Crow* (1965). These are the collections from which the set poems are taken. Further collections followed.

In 1952, Rosemary married Alec Bolton, a fellow-employee of Angus and Robertson. They had three children. Between 1966 and 1971, they lived in London while Alec ran the editorial department of Angus and Robertson. They returned to Australia in 1971 because they wanted their children to grow up Australian.

Rosemary wrote little poetry during their time in London but she was able to travel in Europe and enhance her love and knowledge of art. Her ekphratic poems reference many great works of art.

Alec began work in Canberra at the National Library in 1971. He set up Brindabella Press and Rosemary worked with him as an editor and proof reader. In 1996, Alec Bolton died.

Rosemary Dobson was honoured with the Order of Australia in 1987. She also won the Patrick White Award for poetry. She is remembered as a highly regarded Australian poet who received many accolades and awards and went on to publish hundreds of poems. She published sixteen volumes of poetry in her lifetime. Dobson died in Canberra in 2012, aged 92. Her writing spanned over seventy years.

CONTEXT

Literary/Historical Context

Rosemary Dobson (1920-2012) is said to have had a life-long interest in European culture, especially the paintings of the masters. This interest is reflected in some of her poems set for study. Elizabeth Lawson claimed Dobson's early painting poems, poems which make intertextual reference to the work of painters, "concern the capacity of art to speak across centuries into the reader's present with fresh immediacy." This quote highlights rediscovery, an aspect of discovery in that texts produced in one context and form, can be reinvented to speak to new audiences. This idea is captured in the words,

Old Painting and old poems

Find distant destinations

Can seed new songs

In another language.

Translations under the Trees

(Lawson in *Rosemary Dobson a Celebration* ed. Joy Hooton for Friends of the National Library Australia, Canberra 2000.)

Consider these ideas and align them with the technique of ekphrasis (writing based on artwork) when looking at some set poems. Lawson's words link well to aspects of Discovery as seen in the rubric, particularly, "the experience of discovering something for the first time or rediscovering something that has been lost, forgotten or concealed." They should also help you consider how ideas encountered in your prescribed text convey the concept of Discovery.

Throughout her life, Dobson lived in close contact with other creative people – artists, poets and authors of all kinds. Her own work blossomed in this context.

Whilst never wavering in her sense of herself as an Australian, her art always looked to Europe as a source of inspiration. Rosemary Dobson was interested in exploring the relationship between Australia and its European influences.

Her work is said to examine the balance between dualities – the past and the present, consistency and variety, tradition and innovation, culture and the mundane, reserve and passion, light and dark, myth and reality and the relation of all of these dualities to the 'duality' of Australia and Europe. You may well make your own discoveries regarding many of these aspects in the set poems.

Dobson's use of juxtaposition or balanced contrast, points towards "renewed perceptions", a phrase from the Discovery rubric. You are well advised to incorporate the rubric into your response and ensure you use this study guide to complement rather than replace your own engagement with the set poems.

Does Australia stand for the present, variety, innovation, passion, the mundane and reality in these dualities and Europe for the past, consistency, tradition, reserve, culture, and myth? Or is it even more complex than this? Where are the discoveries?

We will look to Dobson's poetry for answers.

READING JOURNAL

When you study each set poem complete the reading journal template to help your understanding. Use your Journal summaries for revision and essays. Ensure you complete a journal page or pages for EACH poem set for study. If you repeatedly copy the template opposite onto A3 paper, you will have plenty of room to write. Attach the summaries to your bedroom walls and read through them every night. This is a good way to learn your poems and quotes.

It is important to study each poem separately and to consider each poem against the rubric or prescriptions. Then, when you have completed your study of the set poems, it is advised that you compare and contrast them in order to look for similarities and differences relating to the topic of Discovery.

POEM'S TITLE -
POEM'S CONTENT/SUBJECT MATTER : (what the poem is about)
THEMES/MESSAGE(S)/MAIN IDEAS WITH QUOTES/EXAMPLES
RELATIONSHIP TO DISCOVERY/QUOTE(S) FROM RUBRIC AND KEY TECHNIQUES
MY THOUGHTS/ LIKES/ DISLIKES/ ISSUES and LINKS TO OTHER SET POEMS and RELATED TEXT or TEXTS

'YOUNG GIRL AT A WINDOW'

This three stanza poem was published in 1944 in, *In a Convex Mirror*. Dobson was twenty four at the time of publication. It is addressed to a young girl who is physically looking out of a window and metaphorically 'looking out at life'. It may well seem that she is on the threshold of Discovery.

The girl is urged, "Lift your hand to the window latch". This instruction is forcing the girl to consider, at least, opening the latch of the window. Is this to better see out, to remove the barrier of the window that lies between the young girl and life? Whatever the reason for the advice, it is not taken and the persona, "Sighing", decides to, "turn and move away". The girl does not open the window.

The reference to the crossing of "mortal swords" is a reference to conflict, and is usually seen in a Biblical or medieval context. The important thing here, however, is the ambiguity of "crossed'" – swords might be crossed, but so are thresholds. The young girl is about to cross a threshold. The window ledge serves as a liminal space, symbolising the potential for new discoveries.

"The fading air is stained with red" could be a reference to the sunset, as it fades and is red in colour. It might also suggest menstruation. In the next line, though, it definitely becomes a reference to the colour of blood. It makes physical the abstract notion of the killing of Time.

Time is repeated into the first line of the second stanza: "Or Time was lost." In the clock on the wall, "the guiltless minute hand is still", suggesting that time has stopped. Thus, the minute hand is "guiltless" as it is not contributing to the passing of time and its accompanying decay. This is an attempt to hold the moment, to defeat Time. This sense of entrapment, of Time and of childhood within the room is reflected in the tight structure and regular rhyme scheme of the poem.

The room and the light are both personified and then made "hosts to you this final night." The word "final" suggests, again that something is ending, that the young girl is on a threshold of some sort. Presumably this is the threshold between girlhood and womanhood and between childhood and adulthood.

The image of the clock is picked up in "the gently-turning hills" that replace the turning of the minute hand. The girl sees her life spread out before her as seen in the quotation, "Travel a journey with your eyes / In forward footsteps." This is about time, which can only move forward, not back. "This way", that is, in a forward direction, "the map of living lies." The poem then ends with a focus beyond the entrapment of the room and towards the imagined future.

"And this the journey you must go" – the key word is "must". It is the human condition, we have no choice regarding the journey. Life's journey will be, "Through grass and sheaves and, lastly, snow." The images of "grass and sheaves" are images of fertility and growth, while "snow" is the image for winter, a season with connotations of hardship and death.

It has been said that this poem reads as though it may have been based on a painting. This is a definite possibility as Dobson used inter-textual references to artworks in other poems. Whether this is the case or not, the work of art, the painting or the poem, gives the moment a permanence that a real girl, of course, would not have. The text has frozen and metaphorically killed Time, but the girl's destiny is in the final symbolic line of the poem – "and, lastly, snow". This is the metaphoric winter of life and she must journey on towards it.

This may be an ekphratic poem, based on possible art works titled *Girl at the Window* or *Girl at a Window* or even, *Young Woman at a Window*, by European artists including, Dali (1925), Cassatt (1883–4), Gauguin (1888) Greuze (1725–1805), Rembrandt (1651) or even Vermeer. Whether based on an art work or not, Dobson shares with these artists the capture and preservation of a moment through the creation of a text. The adjective 'young' or the word 'girl' in the title suggests there are looming discoveries to be made in life's journey.

There is a duality upon which this poem is based – the capturing of moments in time through art and the written word and the transience of human life. This is a recurring theme in Dobson's work and is significant in that, through capturing a moment, it can be rediscovered by subsequent generations.

Consolidating the Poem's links to Discovery

The poem is about a young girl who is reticent(meaning hesitant) to move outside the known, to discover life. The "window" in the first line represents a barrier between the girl and the world outside and its experiences. Her decision not to open the window "turn and move away" indicates her unwillingness to discover what is out in the world.

The girl is obviously close to making a personal discovery. The reference to "mortal swords" is a reference to conflict and danger, and implies a threat she is not prepared to face. She remains, "On thresholds at the end of day" unwilling to cope with the conflict this discovery will cause in her life.

The references to time in the first and second stanzas,

"Time was killed" and "...Time was lost"

indicate that she is doing all she can to stop this change in her life and the personal discoveries that will accompany it. In the case of art, it alludes to the permanence of art as time is preserved yet reminds the responder that growth and discovery cannot be experienced.

The repetition of "time" and the personification in "time was killed" indicates an attempt to stop the inevitable change that is coming in life. This is an attempt to hold on to childhood, to defeat time and avoid the changes and the discoveries that adulthood will bring in the persona's life.

This idea is further developed by the personification of "The watchful room" which is host to her "this final night." The word "final" implies that the girl's childhood is ending and she fears the changes that becoming a woman will bring. Thus, she fears the changes which lead to self-discovery. The personification also highlights the gentle tone of the poem as other humans seem to have let the girl down. The fact that inanimate objects become her hosts and, ..."nobody spoke and nobody will", highlights that this process of maturation and journeying through life's seasons is a journey of discovery which is taken alone.

Some discoveries cannot be avoided no matter how hard an individual tries. "And this the journey you must go/Through..." The key word used here is "must"- the young girl must take this journey, and make the changes and discoveries associated with the journey. She cannot avoid the human condition and will travel,

"Through grass and sheaves and, lastly snow."

This imagery represents the seasons of the year and of life. It can relate to the aging process.

She has discovered that change cannot be avoided. Thus, Dobson is suggesting that in order to make a self-discovery one must be prepared to take risks and change and this may well be a solitary journey of discovery. There is an implicit understanding that the process of Discovery, as seen in the poem, brings with it positive ramifications such as new understandings and renewed perceptions. The girl's experience may be projected onto your own life as, like the subject, you stand at a similar transformative threshold, that of adulthood.

Questions for 'Young Girl at a Window'

1. What does the window represent in this poem?

2. What is associated with time in this poem?

3. Why is time an important image in this poem?

4. Why do you think the young girl avoids opening the window in the poem?

5. How does the poet suggest the young girl is trying to avoid making changes in her life?

6. How does the poet suggest the young girl will be unable to avoid making changes in her life?

7. What have you learnt about discovery in this poem? Write a paragraph supporting your ideas with close reference to the poem.

8. Suggested activity. Find a copy of Hopkins' poem, 'Spring and Fall' and a copy of John Keats' poem, 'Ode on a Grecian Urn'. What similarities regarding discovery can be made when compared with Dobson's poem? What is the tone, or the composer's attitude, in each poem?

9. Look up some of the listed art works with similar titles. Do you think the poem may be based on a painting? Justify your answer with close reference to the poem and incorporate the term ekphratic in your response.

10. Complete your Reading Journal sheet/sheets for this poem.

'WONDER'

This free verse poem was published in 1948 in the book *The Ship of Ice with Other Poems*. It uses various biblical, artistic and historical references to examine what "wonder is". The conclusion is that wonder is the experience of sheer amazement and near rapture. Einstein's words, quoted at the front of this volume under, 'Scientific and Technological Discovery', define scientific discovery as a, "flight from wonder." It is worth having this opposing thought in mind when considering the poem .

The poem begins by instructing the reader to "turn the page of the book and enter..." Readers are being instructed to enter a world of imagination, a world that is now not literal, a world of art and emotional response. The book contains a reference to "Jan Van Eyck" a Flemish oil painter, artist and portraitist and the poem alludes to his painting *Arnolfini Marriage* (oil, 1434). The painting is described and key features are named in, "...the mirror,/Two figures, a dog". The "soundless room" helps to create a sense of amazement, worldly events do not intrude and we can share the moment captured in the artwork, "five centuries after."

Lazarus, raised to life by Jesus

Dobson then claims that true wonder is "voiceless." As humans we cannot describe what we find wondrous, it can only be felt and "heard in the heart." This idea is reinforced by the biblical reference to Lazarus a man raised to life by Jesus Christ. Humans are unable to explain miracles and so do not try.

"Still dazzled with darkness, turning his face to the wall." This quotation may be seen to contain an intertextual allusion to Hezekiah, in the book of Isaiah and stresses a choice to focus on God rather than the "darkness" or ways of the world. Thus, Lazarus' experience of returning to earthly life from death was transformative and its representation in textual form still causes new generations of responders to wonder over these life and death issues that cannot be explained and have not been discovered by any person still living.

The next reference is to Cortés a 1500s Spanish Conquistador who won Mexico for Spain. Dobson's image of him returning to his "Old World" links with the previous mention of Lazarus. Cortés returns to his old life after his conquests, "Without ovation of guns or trumpets or pennons" unable to describe to others what he has seen and achieved. Both Lazarus and Cortés discovered new worlds, one through a planned expedition and the other unplanned and both were transformed by their experiences.

The final image uses nature to describe the end of life as "a waste of snow" but this does not describe it negatively. In finding the Pole humans cannot describe its beauty and can only look amazed.

The examples in the poem present wonder as a feeling of amazement and awe when contemplating an achievement or discovery whether artistic, spiritual or historical. The reaction of wonder comes in response to a Discovery.

Cortés

Consolidating the Poem's links to Discovery

This poem suggests that wonder and a sense of awe comes about as part of a process of discovery. Dobson suggests that wonder is linked to the experiences that people can never fully understand. Dobson uses the form of poetry to convey the wonder in discoveries linked to various aspects of life and the past. There is a certain paradox here in that wonder is a product of discovery and exists as we cannot fully complete a discovery, through a process of scientific and rational explanation. Thus wonder exists as humans respond to discoveries but cannot fully explain some discoveries.

Dobson is also suggesting that some discoveries cannot be shared because they cannot be verbalised. Using a metaphor, discovery can result in wonder and can take the form of, "music heard in the heart". A complex duality exists in the fact that, despite the distance of time, the existence of the poem or art form, helps others, across time, capture the wonder of the unspoken. This is achieved when the persona claims "(I, also, wordless, was there)".

The idea of being unable to share all discoveries is emphasised in the words, "Wonder...is voiceless" and can only be "heard in the heart." This idea is further reinforced by the biblical reference to Lazarus a man raised to life by Jesus. In a similar way people are still unable to explain miraculous discoveries and so do not try to do so. Lazarus' awe at seeing heaven must have been beyond words. He is, "Still dazzled...turning his face to the wall." Thus, what Dobson is emphasising is that not all discoveries can be shared or told but need to be felt and responded to with a sense of wonder and awe. The words, "intensely meaningful" in the rubric relate to this kind of awe in discovery as does "transformative".

Dobson continues her theme of discovery through history, art and story. She makes a reference to Hernando Cortés a 1500s Spanish conquistador who won Mexico for Spain. Dobson creates an image of him returning to his old life unable to describe the discoveries he has made.

In the final image of the poem Dobson describes the discovery of the Pole "...finding the Pole, with only/Amazement flowering in a waste of snow." Those who discovered the Pole are unable to describe its beauty, they are unable to share their discoveries.

Also relevant is the idea that while the previous examples mentioned are remembered as legacies of individuals, namely Jan Van Eyk, Jesus and Lazarus and Cortés, no one specific scientific explorer or discoverer is mentioned with regard to the discovery of the Pole(s). Hence, the focus shifts to discovery rather than discoverer and this, coupled with the use of present tense in "finding",which is a synonym for Discovering, opens up the concept to all people, across time.

In summary this poem asks readers to make their own discoveries by examining the natural world and the worlds of history, art, religion and literature. Dobson is suggesting that some discoveries, particularly emotional reactions, can only be made by the individual and are unable to be shared with others because humanity does not have the vocabulary to do so and they are deeply personal and moving responses. Thus, she is challenging readers to learn and experience for themselves and therefore make discoveries about the natural world, emotions, art, literature and theology.

This poem is ekphratic in its reference to the Van Eyck painting. It is known that paintings, photographs and portraits depicting other places and people mentioned in the poem exist. They are alluded to within the referenced, "book". Most important, however, is not the specifics of a possible artwork but the sense of awe that can be recaptured despite barriers of time and place, through imagination. Here it is the poem which helps us rediscover lost moments, people, places and significant experiences. Through the four distinct references readers can consider the discovery of love, new places and cultures.

Arnolfini Marriage, oil, 1434, Van Eyck

Although the painting is not named,references in the poem to "('Jan van Eyck was here'), a soundless room,/The windows open, a little late sunlight,the mirror,/Two figures, a dog" point to the poet discovering the painter through this painting. The clues to works of art in Dobson's poems, enable responders to make similar discoveries, across time and place.

Questions for 'Wonder'

1. What does the title of the poem mean and how does it link with the Area of Study?

2. How does Dobson's use of the Van Eyck painting link to the Area of Study? How does she suggest that some discoveries cannot be shared and some can be shared?

3. According to the poet, why are Lazarus' post-death experiences unable to be shared?

4. How is nature used to suggest that some discoveries cannot be shared?

5. What have you learnt about discovery in this poem? Write a paragraph supporting your ideas with close reference to the poem.

6. Complete your Reading Journal sheet/sheets for this poem.

'PAINTER OF ANTWERP'

This poem is about the painter Pieter Breughel the Elder, c. 1525–69, returning to Antwerp from his trip to Italy. Breughel was a Flemish Renaissance painter and printmaker known for his landscapes and peasant scenes (genre painting). He is sometimes referred to as the "Peasant Bruegel." From 1559 he dropped the 'h' from his name and signed his paintings as *Bruegel.* See a sample of his work below.

Dobson describes his head being filled "with...slow wonder" on seeing "... frescoes at Venice and all the odd adventures," such as "Ships in the harbour at Naples with a new rigging/Strangeness enough to empty many tankards." Breughel, was one of a large group of painters to travel to Italy in search of new ideas and styles of art. At the end of the High Renaissance, Antwerp became a seat for painters known as Mannerists, who followed Italian traditions.

The strangeness of new discoveries relating to customs, art and culture are highlighted through the oxymorons, "slow wonder" and "odd adventures." Discovery is, for the painter, a confusing time and the poem's title connects the painters to a place with which he was familiar. The poem highlights the artist distancing himself from new discoveries.

Dobson repeatedly refers to Breughel "plodding" home. She has him discover yet "reject the fanciful" world of the south and return to painting what he knew and understood: the natural world around him, the landscape of the north.

Rejecting the fanciful, and took for a painting

Ploughman, fisherman, and the moon-faced shepherd,

The furrow cut cleanly, the sheep contented

This is the main image in the poem, and in the artwork opposite. It represents Breughel's change in attitude. He is no longer "plodding" home heavily but has made a conscious decision to paint his natural landscapes again. A peaceful tone is created through the words, "cleanly" and "contented". This simple, honest, natural imagery and peaceful tone is used to suggest that Breughel is content in his rejection of the new art world of frescoes and his return to his subject: natural northern landscapes. Thus, discovery of the new and rediscovery of the old is raised within the poem's content.

Icarus was the son of master craftsman Daedalus. Often depicted in art, Icarus and his father attempt to escape from Crete by means of wings that his father constructed from feathers and wax. Icarus' father warns him first of complacency and then of hubris (extreme pride or self-confidence), asking that he fly neither too low nor too high, because the sea's dampness would clog or the sun's heat would melt his wings. Icarus ignored instructions and the melting wax caused him to fall into the sea where he drowned.

Dobson seems to be using this ancient Greek mythological reference to warn readers that it can be better to reject new ideas. Underlying Breughel's journey of discovery is a warning about adopting new forms of art which are filled with foreign themes and ideas. Thus, the story of Icarus is being used as a warning and the poem could be said to have a didactic message relating to Discovery.

Landscape with the Fall of Icarus, oil on canvas, original 1560s. This is now seen as a copy of Brueghel's original."Ploughman, fisherman, and the moon-faced shepherd,The furrow cut cleanly, the sheep contented....Icarus sprawling, two feet out of the sea." Dobson's descriptions are seen in this painting.

Consolidating the Poem's Links to Discovery

This poem is about the painter Pieter Breughel who travelled to Italy. Alliteration, assonance and repetition, seen in "plod homeward" and the reference to him as "peasant" who, "pondering sees the painter at Padua/ In a great plumed hat,..." serves to contrast Breughel with his new experiences and a world of discovery. He stands in contrast to the flashy new sights and sounds he discovered in Italy. The high modality of the first stanza serves to heighten the gulf between Breughel the peasant and the new world he encounters. Similarly negative adjectives such as "slow...odd and queer" and the word "strangeness" heighten the notion that he is uncomfortable and this links to the rubric words which convey that Discovery can be "confronting" and can "challenge individuals". Dobson's poem suggests that not all new discoveries are positive experiences to be embraced.

The second stanza, presented in the past tense, recounts Breughel's rejection of the "fanciful" new sights and sounds and so he returns to what he knows best.

Through use of a mythological intertextual reference to Icarus, Dobson raises the idea of caution regarding new discoveries. Breughel rejected newly discovered art forms and styles encountered in Southern Italy and returned to a style of painting he knew.

In summary Dobson uses some of her favourite images in this poem; images created by unnamed, intertextual references to art. In doing so she is trying to warn readers that not all discoveries are positive and that some discoveries should be rejected in favour of a return to what the individual understands and does well. In identifying the related artwork, responders are involved in a process of discovery and realise that again, this is an ekphrastic poem. In fact, the poem can be seen to be inspired by the Breughel painting, *The Landscape with the Fall of Icarus*. The painting shows not only the fall of Icarus but the central aforementioned image of,

Ploughman, fisherman, and the moon-faced shepherd,

The furrow cut cleanly, the sheep contented

The words, "At the top of the Alps he paused perhaps, looked backwards",/Rejecting the fanciful, and took for a painting", introduces this central image. Here Dobson positions Breughal within the painting and imagines him standing on the top of the Alps, ready to create the work. The words reveal Dobson reflecting on the composition of the painting and positioning the artist in his work as she sees him discover the subject matter for a new painting. Her interpretation of the painting highlights the artist's rediscovery of the values of the north and rejection of the newly discovered values and customs of the South. Thus, a level of metacognition is introduced as Dobson's poem imagines the thinking processes behind the images in this painting. Dobson is discovering the painter behind the work as well as the symbolism and message or theme of the painting. Some say the painting derives from Ovid and it is worth, again, looking for links in terms of journey and self-discovery. Other poets have written on this painting and it may be interesting to compare their discoveries. (See Questions at the end of this section)

Take another look at the reproduction of the painting printed in this booklet and compare the composition of the poem with the content of the poem. You will find a lot of similarities.

While the poem is about Discovery, on a variety of levels, it can also be seen to be about our failure to Discover. In becoming enchanted with the new, we can fail to recognise the value of the old. Like Icarus, in ignoring the wisdom and seeking self-discovery and hubris, we court disaster.

As in `Wonder', this poem may also bring to life the previously quoted words,

Old painting and old poem
Find distant destinations
Can seed new songs
in another language.

Dobson's poem helps us see the painting in a new light. We see Brueghel discovering the world of the south, yet rejecting it and we see the painting rediscovered and reinterpreted through a lens of biographical reflection. Unlike the key subjects of the poem who seemingly fail to notice the fall of Icarus, the poem reminds us to appreciate and fully discover the things about us that are of worth. Dobson's painting poems help responders discover old masters, their works and new meanings

Questions for 'Painter of Antwerp'

1. How does Dobson suggest that the 'Painter of Antwerp' finds the discoveries he has made in Italy strange?

2. Which Breughel painting is central to this poem? Justify your answer.

3. What do you think the main image in the poem is? Why do you believe the image you chose is the main image in the poem?

4. Why does Dobson include an intertextual reference to Icarus?

5. What have you learnt about discovery in this poem? Write a paragraph supporting your ideas with close reference to the poem.

6. Read William Carlos Williams' poem, 'The Landscape with the Fall of Icarus' and W H Auden's, 'Musée des Beaux Arts'. What similarities do you see in terms of the content and interpretation?

7. Research the painting by Breughel and the story of Ovid. You may also like to read Malouf's *An Imaginary Life* and consider it for a related text.

8. Complete your Reading Journal sheet/sheets for this poem.

'TRAVELLER'S TALE'

The 'Traveller's Tale' is told in the first person by a man, who claims to have been an explorer with Columbus. He is looking at artwork by De Bry and remembering his part in the scene depicted in the artwork. The use of "was" in the first line of the poem indicates he is talking about past events in which he claims to have taken part. The fact that his memories involve mythical creatures immediately cause the responder to question the truth of his tale as he seems to have no understanding of which elements of the artwork comprise artistic licence.

In the first section of the poem the persona reveals his confusion between reality and fantasy as he begins to describe some of his adventures. The reference to mythical creatures such as the "cherub" a winged angelic child, being described in biblical tradition as attending on God, demonstrates this confusion.

Similarly mermaids are discussed by the persona. The mermaid was a mythical sea creature with the head and trunk of a woman and the tail of a fish, conventionally depicted as beautiful and with long flowing golden hair. These creatures were said to entice, seduce and confuse men on their long sea voyage. This reference again indicates confusion between reality and illusion.

The persona seems to believe that what is in the artwork is reality and that he was a part of it. He explains that they had a difficult time particularly when the mermaids arrived because they are a symbol of trouble for seamen. Such confusion leads the responder to question whether the persona really participated in sea-faring journeys of discovery or whether the tale is based solely on and derives from the existence of embellished engravings and artwork seen on the walls of the tavern.

Columbus on his way to the New World, An Allegorical Depiction- a copperplate engraving by De Bry showing mermaids, Triton and a conch-shell trumpet. These elements are referenced in the poem. (Courtesy of University of Houston Digital Library)

Triton is portrayed as a mythological Greek God, the messenger of the sea. He is the son of Poseidon and Amphitrite, god and goddess of the sea respectively, and is a herald for his father. He is usually represented as a merman, having the "Triton". Again, such references further reinforce the speaker's difficulty in being able to tell the difference between reality and illusion.

This illusion is continued as he describes the scenes using hyperbole, the "whales...[that] took ...twenty days to sail around" and "...all the scrolls, sir, mixed up with the clouds." The use of overexaggeration coupled with the formal use of "sir" and the speaker's informal register in, "mixed up with" suggest that the speaker is relating a tale to one he aims to impress.

The speaker then asks for "the same again" which means that he wants another drink. This probably indicates that he has been drinking for a while and perhaps the difficulty in telling the difference between reality and the illusion represented by the artwork is due to alcohol. He then tries to prove that what he has said is true by showing the other party a "jack-knife" claiming to have "slit near thirty heathen at the throat." The fact that the speaker may own a sharp folding pocket knife does not equate to the killings he mentions and the logic is flawed. Thus, ironically, his claim of proof adds further doubt to his tale.

The speaker then adds he was with Columbus. He tells of being on the captain's deck with Columbus when Columbus was on the Isle of Pearls. He describes a scene, probably from the artwork he is looking at, of Indians greeting them.

There is then a break in his monologue but we do not know what the barman has said to him. He thanks him and tells of his adventure at the Isle of Pearls. He refers to the *"Gold Lion"* one of the famous ships in the Spanish Armada in order to prove that he was at the event depicted in the artwork. Ironically, again, in aiming to prove the veracity of his story, anachronism may highlight a lack of accuracy.

De Bry's engraving of The Isle of Pearls

During his third voyage to the Indies in 1498, when reaching the Island of Cubagua, Christopher Columbus called it the "Isle of Pearls." While De Bry's engravings of native North and South Americans were based, not on personal experience, but on paintings, written descriptions, or both, his images reflect his decidedly European bias.

The persona then makes his first actual reference to the creator of the artwork. De Bry (1528 – 27 March 1598) was an engraver, goldsmith and editor who travelled around Europe, starting from the city of Liège in the Prince-Bishopric of Liège (where he was born and grew up), then to Strasbourg, Antwerp, London and Frankfurt, where he settled. De Bry created a large number of engraved illustrations for his books. Most of his books were based on first-hand observations by explorers. De Bry himself, acting as a recorder of information, never visited the Americas. This idea of vicarious experience is echoed in the speaker who reponders assume, has not ventured beyond Europe. It extends to Dobson, the poet, who also relates the tale about the traveller's tale, through the imaginative form of a poem. So, many discoveries are made, either vicariously or through the world of the imagination. Explorers are usually linked to scientific or physical discovery, but not in this instance. Again, duality arises. Historical explorations are usually based on fact but this depiction of historical discovery is based on imagination, mythology and vicarious experience.

Vicarious experience can be a valid form of Discovery. That is, the ability to discover something for oneself, through the experience of others. Ironically, this seems to be the same process which the speaker is using when he is projecting himself into the world of the art work and he even claims to have advised the artist. Rather than just convey knowledge and information the speaker's vicarious experience extends to projection into the work itself and helps responders discover the persona and his delusions. The traveller claims to have known De Bry and to have helped him create the artwork as seen in the direct speech, "Put in a cherub, Will, to blow the wind." He also claims he "showed him how to draw the mermaids..." Dobson's readers, knowing the mythological basis for elements in the art work can surmise the over exaggeration and fantastical claims of the so called traveller. The traveller states that De Bry was very accurate in his artistic representations. The opening line, "It *was* confusing sir", suggests a question which responders see as leading and there is dramatic irony in that the responder and unseen partner in conversation seem to understand more about the speaker than he does himself. This highlights the issue of self-awareness and discovery of character as key aspects related to the form.

The bartender then interrupts. Once again we do not hear what he says but the reply indicates that he has been asked by the barman to give directions. He then takes a final drink. "One for the road? Your health, then. Down the hatch."

Reference to De Bry makes this another ekphratic poem although the inaccuracies, confusion and delusions evident also cause the responder to wonder whether the so called traveller was even accurate in his naming of De Bry as the artist of all the artworks alluded to. He also references "Three-masters those", and states,

"I just forgot/How they got mixed up with the Isle of Pearls,"

The speaker describes another work of art and claims that a leg evident in the artwork belonged to a Spaniard who is blotted out. In this poem his discovery leads to claims of knowledge yet irony lies in the responder's knowledge or discovery that the speaker is deluded. Thus, there are many levels of discovery in this poem, from quest and exploration, to discovery of an artist and artwork, discovery of the value of vicarious experience and revelation of character through the form of dramatic monologue.

Art works by de Bry

Consolidating the Poem's Links to Discovery

'Traveller's Tale' is a dramatic monologue. It is a poem told in first person by one who claims to have been involved in explorations in the 'Age of Discovery'. The form of the poem, a dramatic monologue is an important element when linking this poem to the concept of Discovery. Like the monologues of another famous poet, Robert Browning, Dobson's monologues help the reader to discover a lot about the speaker.

The traveller begins by explaining how difficult life was for the early explorers. He explains that "I and Columbus, sir, we stride the deck," thus he placing himself on a ship with the early explorer. He indicates, through the use of mythological creatures, including the "cherub," "Triton" and "mermaids" that life was an exciting adventure but also extremely dangerous. His ignorance of the mythological creatures on the artwork inform the reader that his traveller's tales are doubtful.

Dobson alludes to engravings by Theodorus de Bry who became famous for his depictions of early European expeditions to the Americas, and his art forms the basis for this ekphrastic poem. The verisimilitude of many of de Bry's illustrations is questionable; not least because he never crossed the Atlantic. So too, in claiming to have seen the mythic elements incorporated on the engraving, the traveller's tale is questionable and even comic. Delusion is confirmed through claims such as the speaker's assurance that the artist captured the mermaids in a "lifelike" form. The humour and irony of this is seen as mermaids are mythical creatures.

The first illustration in this section matches images referred to in the poem and is termed an allegory. Similarly, the Tavern setting and the speaker's fondness for a drink serve to help the reader discover much about the persona which is, in fact, not directly stated.

As he speaks in the bar the persona reveals his belief that artwork can help people discover what life was like in the past. He refers to De Bry's artwork and that of three other masters which are presumably hanging on the wall of the tavern. De Bry created a large number of engraved illustrations and prints. Most of his books were based on first-hand observations by explorers and the traveller claims to have known the engraver and to have helped create the artwork through his advice, seen in the direct speech, "Put in a cherub, Will, to blow the wind."

Ironically, the previously mentioned claim to have seen mythological images reveals that the traveller has not really experienced the life of a sailor and seafarer. In light of such inaccuracy, the phases, "The things I've seen I doubt if you'd believe"and "De Bry's the fellow, Sir, that done the prints/ And got it very accurate," can only be seen as ironic. Apart from the speaker revealing ignorance over the content of the art, he makes a reference to "Will" when it was not De Bry's Christian name. The discovery for the responder is that the persona was not really a discoverer in his own right, nor does it seem that he knew De Bry. The speaker's tale is perhaps more of a tall tale than a traveller's true tale.

The traveller's request for "The same again" and "One for the road" suggests that perhaps the traveller is inebriated and therefore unable to tell the difference between fantasy and reality. Dobson also wants readers to appreciate art and what it can teach us but here she displays the "edge of wit" which Susan Sheridan, writing from Flinder's University, recognised in some of Dobson's poems. Dobson's painting poems clarify that there may be many discoveries linked to art.

The rubric states, "By synthesising perspectives, students may deepen their understanding of the concept of discovery." This is true of the effect of this poem in relation to the concept, Discovery. We are left with "renewed perceptions of others", perhaps both of Dobson as a poet, de Bry as an artist and of the legitimacy of the speaker and his tale.

Questions for 'Traveller's Tale'

1. What form does the poem take? Why is this significant?

2. What is the importance of the references to mythology?

3. Why is the setting important?

4. Who was De Bry? Why is his artwork significant here?

5. What is the *"Gold Lion"*? Why is it a noteworthy image in the poem?

6. What have you learnt about discovery in terms of illumination in this poem? Write a paragraph supporting your ideas with close reference to the poem.

7. Look up Browning's poem, 'My Last Duchess' and explain how the form of a Dramatic Monologue and an ekphrastic poem can be linked to this set poem and to discovery.

8. Complete your Reading Journal sheet/sheets for this poem.

'THE TIGER'

This poem, published in 1950, uses an extended metaphor of a caged tiger and the poem identifies the tiger as, "...the poet's furious mind." The tiger is described as "pacing up and down" in captivity and is obviously distressed. The alliteration of the plosive "b" in "Behind the black bars..." adds to the sense of frustration and anger, felt by the captive, pacing tiger. This frustration mirrors the frustration which is a part of the creative process.

The tiger "is behind the black bars of the page." The unexpected use of the word "page" represents the poet's subject matter being trapped. In the use of the word "page" rather than "cage," Dobson transforms the image of the tiger into the metaphorical image of a poet having difficulty capturing meaning and transposing what is felt and experienced into words.

What the poet wants to say is placed,"behind the black bars." These black bars are the lines of print the author uses to communicate ideas. There is the suggestion that, in the same way that the tiger is caged, the poet's subject matter is caged by the limitations of the page. It is, "Captive within the lines of type" and no longer part of a larger context, once found in, "The world where he was free to range". This frustration at being contained, can lead to fury.

Dobson has used a lyrical, regular rhythm to write this poem. The structure mirrors the subject matter and theme of restriction and constraint. There is a four stanza structure with a clear a,b,a,c rhyme scheme.

In the second stanza Dobson uses the tiger's captivity to continue to argue that the poet is constantly searching for a way to overcome the restrictions associated with the writing of poetry. This is seen in the words, "He seeks, and yet can never find". The persona wants a place where, like the tiger, she is "... free to range."

In the third stanza the sustained metaphor of the tiger is used to show the extent of the search for the right words . Using the idea of hunting "the darkness down", she suggests that her search for the right words has taken her to very difficult and distressing places. In the same stanza she suggests that she has achieved perfection previously and so knows what it is like to produce the perfect words, just as the tiger knows what it is like to experience hunting in the wild. "He rakes the sky of stars and hunts" suggests that the tiger will not give up searching for freedom, despite being held in captivity. The harsh sibilance further reinforces the pain both the poet and tiger feel in their captivity.

In the final stanza Dobson repeats her idea that the tiger was once free just as the matter that inspired the poem was free. She gives the power to the readers of her poetry, challenging responders to find the true meaning of her words "Reader, unlock the lines and face/The splendid danger of his rage!" Through the oxymoron of "splendid danger" she also warns her readers about the dangers of knowing the truth. Like the tiger, the truth contained in words can be both powerful and potentially dangerous. The unlocking of words through literacy and the mere act of reading can also be a way to view the poem in terms of the concept.

The main idea in this poem is symbolised by the central extended metaphor: that of the caged tiger. It may represent the restricted ideas of the poet. "Behind the black bars of the page" is one of the key lines in the poem. The use of the word "page" instead of "cage", which one would expect, represents the poet's inspiration caged or trapped within a poem. The use of the word "page" transforms the tiger into a metaphorical image of a writer having difficulty creating his/her poetry. Thus, the main idea in the poem may be interpreted as the poet's frustration at being unable to truly discover his/her voice and express ideas clearly to the audience.

This poem is one of self-discovery for the poet. She is constantly trying to find a way to overcome the restrictions writing poetry presents. She wants a place where, like the tiger, she is "...free to range."

Dobson discovers that she is unable to achieve this freedom alone. She must allow readers to interpret the poetry themselves and she challenges readers to find the real meaning in her words no matter how confronting they may be.

Reader, unlock the line and face

The splendid danger of his rage!"

Within the paradox "splendid danger" there is also a warning to readers about the danger and exhilaration of discovering and knowing the truth. A D Hope coined the oxymoron "passionate serenity", to describe Dobson's work and within the passion of this image, there is a calm message. Dobson presents a troubling emotion, Truth. Thus, there is also self-discovery for readers; we must recognise that the truth is both powerful and potentially dangerous. People must consider that a word either spoken or written can be dangerous and can capture the truth or present falsity. Hence, as responders we must either accept Dobson's challenge, and therefore discover the truth contained in her words, or choose not to, leaving the metaphorical tiger caged.

Dobson seems self aware, indeed, she has made the discovery that, as a poet, she captures ideas, emotions and concepts. By unlocking the content of poetry through interpretation and thinking more broadly on the poet's subject matter, responders are able to make discoveries for themselves and go beyond the confines of the poet's trapped words on a page. The metaphor of the tiger as representative of the poet's mind and/or the content of the poem, serves to support this view. This interpretation links to responders' learning and the poem serves as a catalyst for personal discovery and causes responders to reflect on knowledge gained through the written word.

Questions for 'The Tiger'

1. What is the significance of the use of the word "page" in the second line of the poem?

2. Who or what do you think "the tiger" represents in this poem?

3. Why does Dobson believe she must give power to the readers of her poetry?

4. What is the most significant technique used in this poem? Explain your decision.

5. What have you learnt about discovery in this poem? Write a paragraph supporting your ideas with close reference to the poem.

6. Complete your Reading Journal sheet/sheets for this poem.

'COCK CROW'

The title is originally from the Hebrew and refers to the beginning of the day or dawn when the cock traditionally crows. It is also a biblical reference when Jesus prophesied that Peter would betray him thrice (three times) before the cock crowed twice. Mark 14: 66-72 is the Bible reference for this story. You are advised to look it up and read it.

The emphasis on individuality in the poem is established at the beginning of the poem through the speaker desiring to "be myself, alone." She has left other people behind in the "lit house" to spend time by herself with her thoughts. The suggestion is that she is overwhelmed by what is going on in the house and needs to escape. The use of the word "house" rather than home suggests she feels a lack of connection to the place and the people in it at that moment.

"Three times I took that lonely stretch/Three times..." The repetition of "three" could simply suggest that the persona has a lot of troubling thoughts to deal with, but the use of "thrice" in the last stanza suggests she is betraying someone or perhaps even betraying herself through the biblical allusion to Peter's betrayal of Jesus. In leaving the house she has, temporarily at least escaped her responsibilities "...absolved me of my bonds."

CHRIST APPEARING TO SAINT PETER

In the third stanza, the responder leaves her mother and daughter in the house, denying them to meet her own need of isolation. She, "...denied/Their needs in shutting the door." The persona's obvious need for isolation and personal space is clear. Dobson, wrote about a woman, both mother and daughter, leaving the house to "escape her bonds." The poet herself commented to McCooey in an interview, that this poem, "expressed the dilemma of the creative person who has human responsibilities that must be met". Dobson noted that it seemed to be an idea that many had overlooked. Such themes are relevant to feminist literary criticism and the conflict between a women's discovery of self and demands of roles may be explored.

The persona needs solitude to organise her thoughts. Her responsibilities have become too much for her to cope with, they have become a burden to her. Paradoxically, in the fourth stanza, she also acknowledges her deep love for her family; they are a part of her. This is seen in the poignant image, "And love that grows about the bone."

"Too brief illusion!" This phrase indicates that the isolation cannot continue. The exclamation mark indicates the persona's frustration at not being able to continue to be alone and the realisation that she is abdicating her responsibilities. The use of "thrice" in this final stanza rather than three, coupled with the title and the cock crow in the final stanza, establishes the biblical allusion to Peter's betrayal of Jesus. (Mark 14: 66-72). Like Peter the cock had crowed "thrice" as she walked along the road, three times denying her responsibility to her family by refusing to return to the house. In doing so she was able to hold on to the fantasy of her independence.

And turned the handle of the door

Thinking I knew his meaning well.

The persona can no longer deny her responsibilities; like Peter she comes to the realization of what she has "thrice" denied. She returns home to meet her responsibilities.

Consolidating the Poem's Links to Discovery

There are two main ideas in this poem. The first idea is established at the beginning of the poem in the persona's desire to "be myself alone." The persona of the poem has made a personal discovery: that is, she needs to abandon her responsibilities and be alone for a while. She is overwhelmed by her responsibilities. She has no emotional connection at this point to what is going on as indicated by her use of the noun "house" rather than home which is a more emotive term.

The fact that Dobson uses the biblical image of Peter's betrayal of Jesus suggests the persona feels some guilt in leaving her responsibilities behind in the house. In the third stanza responders realise the reason for this guilt; she has left her mother and daughter in the house.

"My mother and my daughter slept."

In her isolation the persona discovers, paradoxically, that she loves her mother and daughter. She describes the extent of the love in the image, "And that love grows about the bone" but in her guilt there is also the personal discovery that she needs more personal time and isolation, more time to "escape her bonds."

There is another personal discovery made by the persona in this poem. The realisation is that she cannot remain free of her responsibilities. "Too brief illusion!" The exclamation mark indicates the persona's frustration at having to return to the house and deal with her responsibilities. There is also an acceptance of the responsibilities her mother and daughter represent.

The second main idea involves the personal discovery made by the poet. As the previous quote from an interview with Dobson indicates, the personal could be seen as Dobson trying to escape her responsibilities to find the time and space to write. This would create a personal dilemma for a creative person needing the time and space to produce, yet having the responsibilities of a daughter and mother. The existence of the poem indicates that she continues to produce her art, despite her family responsibilities and her frustration regarding the act of creating her art. There is a sense of the persona betraying both herself as an artist and her family within this poem.

Questions for 'Cock Crow'

1. Is Dobson's use of religious imagery effective in this poem? Why or why not?

2. Could the poem be a metaphorical representation of part of Dobson's life? Support your answer with evidence.

3. What is the significance of the poet's use of the word "house" rather than "home"?

4. What self-discoveries does the persona make in this poem?

5. Is the persona of the poem obliged to return to her responsibilities? Why?/Why not? Support your answer with close textual reference to the poem.

6. What have you learnt about discovery in this poem? Write a paragraph supporting your ideas with close reference to the poem.

7. Read Gwen Harwood's 'In the Park'. Compare the two poems and reflect on similarities and differences as they relate to the concept of self discovery and familial responsibilities.

8. Complete your Reading Journal sheet/sheets for this poem.

'GHOST TOWN: NEW ENGLAND'

The setting for the poem is anticipated in the title of the poem which refers to the northern New South Wales region of New England. The inappropriateness of the term, "New England" is evident in Dobson's image of the intense dry heat of summer in Australia, which is so unlike England.

Dobson creates a visual image of the colour and life being removed from the grass by the heat of the sun in the first image of the poem, "The grass is bleached by the summer sun". The alliteration of the "s" in the first image and the sustained sibilance in the words, "pods rustle", seen in the second, auditory image adds to the harshness of the tone. Such harshness is further emphasised through the choice of the adjective, "dry".

In the next image Dobson is suggesting even nature, betrayed by itself, struggles to survive in this harsh land. She conveys this sense of struggle and betrayal through a simile and personification which suggest timidity, uncertainty and contrast in,

On Quartz-bright rocks the lichens creep

Like frail anemones betrayed

Still trembling towards an unknown sea.

The wind is both violent and paradoxically life giving in the final image of the stanza. It assists by scattering the seeds and there are connotations of fertility, yet we realise that these are "seeds of light" and hence, not productive.

Having established the scene of a harsh landscape for the poem, the persona stops due to the physical danger created by the

"Knife-edge... scree". A scree is an area of small stones that are very unstable and could cause a person to slip into the "plunging scarps" below. Her imagination allows her to go possibly to hell, suggested by the "shroud" mentioned in the previous image. This hellish image is further enhanced by the repetition of the persona's eyes dropping down "to find at last the dry creek-bed." The image of a lifeless area is further enhanced as is the idea of a descent into hell.

The third stanza suggests that someone looking at this landscape must be realistic about the area.

> *This is no landscape for the eye*
>
> *Cupped by a hand to shield the mind*

The persona must accept the harshness of, "...earth's most naked cruelty" in this land.

Dobson is also challenging the responder to accept the harsh truth of their lives in this section of the poem. We must be like the "eagle-hawk", another name for the Australian Wedge-tailed eagle, and continue to investigate and explore our lives with both the courage and clear eye sight provided by the hawk. Thus, Dobson is using the setting of the ghost town as a metaphor for a real analysis of life, accepting both its disappointments and its endeavours.

In the fourth stanza Dobson has the persona imagine how the townspeople lived when the town was occupied. She suggests the town was once alive and filled with people who had hopes and dreams which were destroyed by the harsh reality of the landscape. The new England town had plantings of "oak" and "hedge" which are plants traditionally associated with England rather than Australia and they are not best suited to the dry barren environment. Pathetic fallacy is used as the harsh barren landscape reflects the subject matter of the dead town. Hopes and dreams the people had for recreating a town, as in England, were dashed. Dobson uses this image metaphorically to further challenge responders to face the reality of life with honesty and courage.

In the fifth stanza Dobson returns to the reality of the town, challenging responders to face, yet again, the reality of their lives. The verb "lean" in, "The houses lean against the wind" suggests a collective resistance but, ultimately, the poem reasserts nature, destroying man's hopes and dreams. The houses' eyes are also "...scarfed with sheets of tin". Personifying the houses and then suggesting that the tin is stopping the house from seeing the landscape clearly raises a challenge. Metaphorically this challenges responders to see their surroundings as they are and to accept reality.

The stanza suggests that there is no life left in the town, the bell no longer calls the people to church, and the door "shuts on nothing." The final two lines of the stanza "...sick unease/I saw a child's discarded shoe" suggest that rather than a slow destruction there was some event that caused the town to be vacated quickly. There is a cumulation of negative adjectives such as, "cracked complaining, sick, discarded" which covey lost potential.

The final stanza begins with a rhetorical question. This question asks if, in going on with their lives unthinkingly, the townsfolk caused the destruction of the town. This rhetorical question provides the culmination of the metaphorical meaning of the poem. It suggests that continuing with a life full of pride can cause humanity to be destroyed.

In the final two lines Dobson suggests people would rather not face reality,

> *His mind, as mine, will veer away*
>
> *Who lacks the hawks' unwavering eye.*

Ignorance, arrogance and lack of perception will cause destruction and this may be a gem of truth and nugget of discovery which is embedded in the content and message of the poem. Texts offer themes and messages and understanding these are a form of Discovery for readers. By continuing to live their lives believing they can defeat nature, people will inevitably defeat themselves. Thus, Dobson challenges people, (particularly Christians) to face life as it really is, metaphorically in terms of "the hawks' unwavering eye." The reference to "the fall" works on several levels meaning the drop to the dry creek bed, the demise of the townsfolk and the arrogance of man in defying God's order and command which ultimately brought death to the human race through Adam and Eve's sin. Here the town itself, has died through a failure to live in harmony with the accepted conditions. Life will bring changed conditions and to thrive we must respond accordingly.

Consolidating the Poem's Links to Discovery

In this poem Dobson helps readers discover the harshness of Australian history, landscape, climate and lifestyle. She does this by showing the destruction of a small town in rural New England.

Dobson creates an image of the town struggling to survive and failing, in the harsh natural setting to help readers learn, and discover, how difficult life was, and still is, in rural Australia. She achieves a sense of struggle and a failure to adapt to changed conditions through a simile and personification in:

On Quartz-bright rocks the lichens creep

Like frail anemones betrayed

Still trembling towards an unknown sea.]

The idea of lichens creeping like frail sea creatures towards an unknown sea represents the idea of the land betraying the flora and also reinforces the need to adapt to changing conditions. The word "still" highlights the ongoing failure to adapt and to accept change. The vegetation reflects the failure to recognise changed conditions as the landscape supposedly changed from sea to desert in central Australia (as indicated by the fossil record).

The image of seeds conveys connotations of life and food. But the image of, "The wind goes scattering seeds of light", helps the reader discover the futility of trying to combat the harsh environment. This discovery revolves around the pun on "...seeds of light", when the expectation would be to read the phrase,"seeds of life". In stanza four, later references to plantings, the bakery and meal and bread all serve to reinforce the strong hopelessness in the fact the seeds are only of light and are thus, tenuous and vacuous and offer no potential for life as hope is scattered.

Dobson also helps readers discover, and learn, how dangerous life could be in rural Australia. She describes a dangerous "Knife-edge...scree" which cannot be cultivated or inhabited by people. She then challenges readers to be realistic about the discoveries made about the Australian landscape, life style and climate. She asks us to discover this for ourselves by being like the "eagle-hawk" and continuing to investigate and explore our own life with the clarity provided by the hawk. This will allow us to discover the truth about life in Australia for ourselves. Thus Dobson is using the setting of the "Ghost Town" as a metaphor for a real analysis of life, challenging people to discover and accept life in rural Australia with both its endeavours and disappointments.

In the fourth stanza Dobson has the persona imagine how the townspeople lived when the town was occupied. She suggests the town was once alive and filled with people who had hopes and dreams which were destroyed by the harsh reality of the landscape. As a result any hopes and dreams the people had were futile. Dobson uses this image metaphorically to further challenge responders to face the reality of life with honesty and courage. Acceptance of reality is a part of self-discovery.

The harshness of life in Australia is emphasised in the knowledge that this rural town in New England is a ghost town. In presenting this image, Dobson is helping readers learn, and discover, that Australia is nothing like England in terms of climate or life style. In the fifth stanza Dobson states that there is no life left in the town. The structures have been left "lean[ing] against the wind," and the church bell no longer calls the people to church.

In the final stanza Dobson challenges readers to discover their own role in the destruction of small towns in rural Australia. She uses the rhetorical question:

Was it on such a summer's day

They gathered from the bakery,

The store, the church, and, beckoned on

By the compulsion of the fall,

Plunged to those knife-edged silences?

to provide the culmination of the metaphorical meaning of the poem. It challenges readers to recognise or discover how continuing with a life full of pride can cause humanity to be destroyed.

In the final two lines of the poem, after challenging readers to discover the truth about the history of rural Australia, Dobson suggests that humanity would rather not act on the discoveries they have made.

His mind, as mine, will veer away

Who lacks the hawk's unwavering eye.

Thus Dobson challenges people to learn from the discoveries of Australian history and accept the reality of the harshness of the Australian climate and lifestyle. She challenges us to question and learn from the past. This is a poem which links to expectations and discovery. The title implies expectations based on past traditions and the poem expands on the importance of discovering current conditions and responding to them. We are urged to be discerning and respond to the truth of situations, rather than the expectations we may have of them.

Discovering a Broader Reading

The poem, like a crime story, presents readers with a mystery and inherent in this is the concept of discovery. Apart from the Australian context, presented in the reading above, it is interesting to consider the setting of New England, on the East coast of America. This area also has ghost towns and some definitions of Eagle Hawk, define the birds as any numerous American birds of prey. Like the British in Australia, the English settlers in America also faced a different climate and dangers in the form of Indian attacks. The violent image of 'knife edged silences', the troubling and confronting visual image of the "child's discarded shoe" and the reference to "earth's most naked cruelty" enables us to see this poem through the lens of a convex mirror and thus, broaden our interpretation. We can discover generalities from a specific example. Thus, although essentially Australian, the message of the poem may be applicable to a broader audience and be seen from alternate contextual perspectives. We are challenged as readers to question mystery within texts and to seek, through analysis, to discover meaning. Here we are challenged, in a general sense, to discover and respond to situations and adapt to them in order to survive. There is an imperative to discover and respond accordingly or perish.

Questions for 'Ghost Town: New England'

1. What type of discoveries are explored in this poem?

2. How does Dobson suggest that life rural Australia is very different from life in rural England?

3. How does Dobson suggest that life in rural Australia is harsh?

4. What is the significance of the image of "the hawks' unwavering eye?"

5. Why is the Australian setting of the poem significant?

6. What discoveries can readers make from History? Support your answer with close reference to the poem.

7. What have you learnt about discovery in this poem? Write a paragraph supporting your ideas with close reference to the poem.

8. List some similarities and differences regarding Discovery and environment as presented in, 'Ghost Town: New England' and 'Painter of Antwerp'.

9. Barbara Kingsolver's novel *The Poisonwood Bible* contains a character, the father, who clings to old ways and rejects new discoveries which are more aligned to a changed environment. The novel is lengthy but may prove an interesting related choice. The narrative style also links well to this Area of Study.

10. Complete your Reading Journal sheet/sheets for this poem.

THE ESSAY

The essay has been the subject of numerous texts and you should have the basic form well in hand. As teachers, the point we would emphasise would be to link the paragraphs both to each other and back to your argument (which should directly respond to the question). Of course, ensure your argument is logical and sustained.

Make sure you use specific examples and that your quotes are accurate. To ensure that you respond to the question make sure you plan carefully and are sure what relevant point each paragraph is making. Topic sentences are helpful to begin each paragraph and it is solid technique to actually 'tie up' each paragraph by linking it to the question.

When composing an essay the basic conventions of the form are:

- Address the question, state your argument, outline the points to be addressed and perhaps have a brief definition.

↓

A solid structure for each paragraph is:

- Topic sentence (*the main idea and its link to the previous paragraph/ argument*)
- Explanation/ discussion of the point including links between texts if applicable.
- Detailed evidence (*Close textual reference- quotes, incidents and technique discussion.*)
- Tie up by restating the point's relevance to argument/ question

↓

- Summary of points
- Final sentence that restates your argument

As well as this basic structure you will need to focus on:

Audience – for the essay the audience must be considered formal unless specifically stated otherwise. Therefore, your language must reflect the audience. This gives you the opportunity to use the jargon and vocabulary that you have learnt in English. For the audience ensure your introduction is clear and has impact. Avoid slang or colloquial language including contractions (doesn't, eg, etc).

Purpose – the purpose of the essay is to answer the question given. The examiner evaluates how well you can make an argument and understand the module's issues and its text(s). In the case of the Area of Study, markers look for a deep conceptual understanding and you must reveal understanding using examples from your prescribed text and a related text or texts. An essay is solidly structured so its composer can present ideas with clarity. This is where you earn marks. Essays do not retell the story of a text or state the obvious. They analyse rather than describe.

Communication – Take a few minutes to plan the essay. If you rush into your answer it is almost certain you will not make the most of the brief 40 minutes to show all you know about the question. More likely you will include irrelevant details that do not gain you marks but waste your precious time. Remember an essay is formal so do not do the following: story-tell, list and number points, misquote, use slang or colloquial language, be vague, use non sentences or fail to address the question.

HSC STYLE ESSAY QUESTION

Remember that essay responses must respond to essay questions and when you submit a practice essay, it should have a question written at the top. Start by underlining the key words in the question.

The Concept of Discovery may be conveyed differently in and through texts, but the result for responders is a deeper understanding of self and the world.

Discuss this statement with close reference to your prescribed text and two related texts.

PLAN

Introduction Start by introducing the texts you are using in your essay response ***Argument:*** The BOSTES definition for Discuss is to -Identify issues and provide points for and/or against. Consider using differing textual forms which affect how the concept of Discovery is conveyed. For example, a film will convey the concept of Discovery using visual, filmic techniques whereas a novel will use narrative techniques. Using a variety of textual forms will enable you to argue for the first half of the statement and enable you to show the different ways discovery is conveyed. Also consider the rubric and reflect on the different ways Discovery can be and is presented in your texts.	You need to let the marker know what texts you are discussing. You can start with a definition but it can come in the first paragraph of the body. You MUST state your argument in response to the question and the points you will cover as part of it. Don't wait until the end of the response to give it!

Do not forget the second part of the question, that is, the link to you as a responder and your deeper understanding of self and the world, through studying Discovery. You may like to argue that although forms and text types differ and aspects of Discovery raised in and through texts differ, it is this variety which helps you as a responder relate the concept to your own understanding of the world and your place in it.

- (Aim to incorporate discussion of techniques when discussing text and making close textual references.)

↓

Idea 1– Look to the rubric and identify what kinds of Discovery are raised in your texts.

Idea 2- Explore how these are raised, through selected form and relevant techniques.

Idea 3 - Analyse their impact in terms of discovery on you as a responder. Is it a bildungsroman text. Do characters make personal discoveries, grow and learn? Is the composer him or herself a factor linked to a responder and discovery? Look at the purpose in writing the text. Explore these ideas in both your prescribed and related text or texts. In what ways have the aspects of Discovery raised in the three text enhanced your understanding of yourself and the world?

Ideas can be expanded into several paragraphs. be sure to set out paragraphs clearly using a topic sentence, explanation, examples and analysis of examples in terms of technique and link to question.

↓

Finally, your conclusion should incorporate a summary of key ideas. Do not raise new points in a conclusion.

- Provide a final sentence that restates your argument

Make sure your conclusion restates your argument. It does not have to be too long.

DISCOVERY: SUGGESTED RELATED TEXTS

You are often advised to select related texts that do not mirror the form of your Prescribed text. In addition, you are reminded to select related material wisely and look for links to the rubric, the concept and to highlight similarities and differences with prescribed material. Markers have noted that the judicious selection of related material is a key factor when evaluating responses. Sophisticated texts when well analysed in relation to the concept, and strongly analysed in relation to the prescribed text, will impress markers more than texts you may have happened to read at school in previous years in Stage Four or Five.

In the following list, categories are used for convenience but titles are not always exclusive to genre or text type. Many hybrid texts exist which cross boundaries of genre.

PROSE-FICTION/NON FICTION

Bypass – The Story of a Road by Michael McGirr

About one man's journey of discovery along the Hume Highway between Sydney and Melbourne. This is a hybrid text which is part travelogue, memoir, history and romance.

Gulliver's Travels by Jonathan Swift

This classic tale is about Gulliver's discovery of Lilliput. Through his arduous adventures he discovers lessons about society and humanity. The tale is a satirical view of the state of European government, and of petty differences between religions. It addresses the origins of human corruption, the conflict between Lilliputians and Yahoos, and other races.

A History of Reading by Alberto Manguel

Discover a personal response to books and reading and a love of literature. This is a wonderful non-fiction text written by an award winning author.

Looking for Alibrandi by Melina Marchetta

The aspect of discovery here is Alibrandi discovering who her estranged father is, as well as coping with various teenage issues in high school. This text is not as sophisticated as some other choices but it does raise aspects of culture and personal discovery.

Memoirs of a Geisha by Arthur Golden

This novel is about personal discovery and the development of identity in a tumultuous period in Japanese history.

The Secret River by Kate Grenville

Discover the interaction between the white settlers and the Aboriginal population on the Hawkesbury River. The discovery centres on place, people, including the composer, and cultures.

Small Island by Andrea Levy

Told by four narrators, the novel is set during the Second World War and tells the story of four different lives. There is racial tension and discovery of what it is like living with someone who comes from a different part of the world. Not only do you discover this new way of life, but it brings about a discovery of the self.

So Much To Tell You by John Marsden

Here a scarred and introverted girl who is an elective mute, discovers a way to reveal her feelings to the reader in the form of a diary. In turn, readers discover Marina's life and relationships as she also discovers non-verbal ways to communicate with others.

Unpolished Gem by Alice Pung

In this text the Discovery theme involves cultural differences, migration and a new life for an Asian family in Footscray, Victoria. This text is about discovering life in a family and about cultures.

An Unsuitable Job for a Woman by P.D. James

Female detective Cordelia Gray investigates a suicide and a family with many secrets. The writing is detailed with plenty of atmosphere and clues. It is a crime fiction text, detection discovery with a twist. Consider other examples of Crime writing as discovery is a key theme within this genre

The Snowman by Jo Nesbo

Detective discovery in a European setting. This text presents modern take on the genre and is very well written.

FICTION / FILM

Alice in Wonderland (novel and film) original by Lewis Carroll

Alice discovers a magical fantasy world where she is in turmoil. Here she has amazing adventures and meets many intriguing characters.

Chronicles of Narnia (novel and film) original by C.S. Lewis

Four children, Peter, Suzan, Edmund and Lucy, discover a magical world behind their wardrobe and learn about their special role in saving the land from a great evil. The form of allegory can help responders discover deeper truths.

The Lost Thing (picture book and film) original by Shaun Tan

A boy discovers a lost thing and journeys to find it a home.

The Never-ending Story (novel and film) original by Michael Ende

The protagonist Sebastian discovers the world of Fantasia which is dying. He becomes part of the book he is reading and saves the world.

Sherlock Holmes (novel and film) original by Conan Doyle

Any of the *Sherlock Holmes* mysteries of adventures such as *The Hound of the Baskervilles* are recommended. These texts present discovery through means of deduction, calculation and scientific reasoning.

Under the Dome by Stephen King (novel and film)

Imagine being trapped and cut off from the world under a dome of power. This is a Science fiction text that is a long read but an intriguing idea. The initial discovery is awesome but then characters begin to discover things about themselves and others.

Where the Wild Things Are (picture book and film) original by Maurice Sendak

A young boy is punished by his mother to go to his bedroom, which transforms into a jungle where he sails to an island and discovers that it is inhabited by malicious beasts known as the "Wild Things." After successfully intimidating the creatures, Max is hailed as the king of the Wild Things and enjoys a playful romp with his subjects. However, he discovers that being king is not all that great. If you select a Picture book, be sure to discuss visual literary techniques in a sophisticated manner.

Wizard of Oz (novel and film) original by Frank L. Baum

Dorothy discovers a magical fantasy world where various characters discover their true character. For example, Tin Man finds his heart.

The Book Thief by Marcus Zusak

A young orphaned girl meets her new family in Germany during the Second World War. Through the focalisation of this young girl the reader pieces together the narration and discovers what is going on in the world around her. Historical discovery.

FILM

The Island directed by Michael Bay

Science fiction film about clones that live in a false utopian prison who discover their true origins as spare organ parts for wealthy but terminally ill people. The revelation is the discovery and how the discoverers respond to it.

It's Kind of a Funny Story directed by Ryan Fleck

A teenage boy checks himself into the mental ward only to find he has been relocated to the adult's ward. The film follows the boy and the friends he makes along the way.

50/50 directed by Jonathan Levine

Adam learns how to cope and live his life by coming to terms with his cancer.

An Education directed by Lone Sherfig

Jenny is in her final year of high school and has high hopes for the future when she meets a middle aged man who shows her another world. Jenny has to decide which world she wants to live in.

Consider also documentaries and other non fiction filmic forms.

POETRY

A suite of poems rather than one single poem is recommended, especially if the poem is brief.

'Easy Does It' by Bruce Dawe

A poem about discovering his boy and how he has to be 'careful' with him.

'Discovery' by Wislawa Szymborksa

The poem begins with 'I believe in the great discovery' and it is about faith and evidence.

'La Belle Dame Sans Merci' by John Keats

A knight discovers a new love and a new faery world but it is not what it seems and his discovery in this poem leads him to a life of misery.

'My Last Duchess' by Robert Browning

A dramatic monologue which reveals chilling and disturbing details about the speaker.

'Spring and Fall – To a Young Child' by Gerard Manley Hopkins

This is an address to a young girl, Margaret, and raises the discoveries that the child will make about the human condition. There is a prediction that these discoveries concerning life and death will be inevitable and with come with age and maturity.

SONGS

Remember that, if you write about a song, you are advised to consider more than just the lyrics.

At Seventeen by Janis Ian

Teen coming of age song about the angst of discovering what and who you are.

Kings and Queens by 30 Seconds to Mars

Discovering empowerment and greatness from despair.

Meant to Live by Switchfoot

Making the most out of life and discovering your absolute potential.

We Won't get Fooled Again by The Who

The persona in the song discovers that the new government which is established after a revolution is the same as the old government, and criticises it.

WEBSITES

100 Questions to Inspire Self-Discovery

HTTP://WWW.ALEXANDRAFRANZEN.COM/2013/04/18/100-QUESTIONS-TO-INSPIRE-RAPID-SELF-DISCOVERY/

Quite a few sites like this one that offer ideas on the topic. Read judiciously.

Discover the Extreme World

HTTP://WWW.MILESKELLY.NET/PRODUCTS-PAGE/DISCOVERY-EXPLORE-YOUR-WORLD/

Read the book blurb: Produced in association with Discovery Channel, this jam-packed book focuses on the extremes of core reference subjects. From animal giants to futuristic spy technology to the deepest caves and coldest places in the Universe. Nice change as it is aimed at children.

Discover Magazine

HTTP://AU.ZINIO.COM/MAGAZINE/DISCOVER/PR-500621662

Science based but has a wide range of articles on all sorts of interesting topics such as foods and environment.

HTTP://WWW.MILESKELLY.NET/PRODUCTS-PAGE/DISCOVERY-EXPLORE-YOUR-WORLD/

Discovery channel

HTTP://WWW.DISCOVERYCHANNEL.COM.AU/

Here you will discover many shows about discovery but it is also about learning.

Discovery Education

HTTP://WWW.DISCOVERYEDUCATION.COM/TEACHERS/

This address will lead you to the teacher resources but the site is full of content that shows another aspect of discovery i.e. education.

Famous People who Made Scientific Discoveries

HTTP://WWW.BIOGRAPHY.COM/PEOPLE/GROUPS/DISCOVERY/SCIENTIFIC

Another excellent source for evidence in film and written form on a comprehensive site.

Kids Discover

iPad app. Below is the address for the preview but you can download the app and use it. Excellent resource.

HTTPS://ITUNES.APPLE.COM/AU/APP/KIDS-DISCOVER/ID574832964?MT=8

The Science Channel

SCIENCE.DISCOVERY.COM/FAMOUS-SCIENTISTS-DISCOVERIES/100-GREATEST-DISCOVERIES.HTM

Almost complete collection of all the scientific discoveries covering most of the ancient and modern worlds in film and clearly explained.

Self Discovery

HTTP://EN.WIKIPEDIA.ORG/WIKI/JOURNEY_OF_SELF-DISCOVERY

Here are some definitions and links to the topic. A useful starting point to develop your ideas.